DATE DUE

ALSO BY CHRISTINA PUGH

Rotary

Gardening at Dusk (chapbook)